The Work of Prayer

James O. S. Huntington

The Work of Prayer

A Manual for Those
Who Would Pray Well

SOPHIA INSTITUTE PRESS®
Manchester, New Hampshire

This 2005 edition of *The Work of Prayer* is a revised version of the fifth edition of the book, published in 1949 by Holy Cross Press, West Park, New York, and includes minor editorial revisions and a collection of daily prayers.

Sophia Institute Press®
Box 5284, Manchester, NH 03108
1-800-888-9344
www.sophiainstitute.com

Library of Congress Cataloging-in-Publication Data

Huntington, James O. S. (Otis Sargent), b. 1854.
The work of prayer : a manual for those who would pray well /
James O.S. Huntington. — Rev. ed.
    p. cm.
ISBN 1-933184-10-8 (pbk. : alk. paper)
1. Prayer — Christianity. I. Title.

BV210.3.H86 2005
248.3'2 — dc22
2005021278

To my mother,
who first taught me to pray

"Pray for my soul. More things are wrought by prayer
Than this world dreams of. Therefore, let thy voice
Rise like a fountain for me night and day.
For what are men better than sheep or goats
That nourish a blind life within the brain,
If, knowing God, they lift not hands of prayer
Both for themselves and those who call them friend?
So is the whole round earth in every way
Bound by gold chains about the feet of God."

Alfred Lord Tennyson

Contents

1. Understand What Prayer Is. 3

2. Understand Who God Is. 13

3. Offer Your Prayer Through Christ 23

4. Let the Holy Spirit Guide Your Prayer 33

5. Fit Prayer into Your Day. 45

6. Begin Your Day with Prayer. 57

7. Devote Time to Mental Prayer 71

8. Pray Throughout the Day 77

9. Be Prepared for Difficulties in Prayer 89

10. Understand Why You Should Pray. 101

⁀

Prayers for Every Day 111

Biographical Note: James O. S. Huntington . . 129

Editor's note: The biblical quotations in the following pages are taken from the Douay-Rheims edition of the Old and New Testaments. Where applicable, quotations have been cross-referenced with the differing names and enumeration in the Revised Standard Version, using the following symbol: (RSV =).

The Work of Prayer

Chapter One

Understand What Prayer Is

"All through this life, in our prayers as in
everything else, we are under a discipline of mystery,
working on little by little towards the world of perfect light
where the mystery will be opened, and the satisfaction
of awaking in the Lord's likeness will be complete."

Frederic Dan Huntington

We belong — for a while — to two worlds. One of these is the world about us, made up of the things that we see and hear and touch and taste and smell, and of similar things at present beyond the reach of our senses. I sit here at the table and look around the room. There are shelves of books, chairs, a case of drawers with a card catalog. Through the windows I see trees against the blue sky, the grass on the lawn below, the roof of a building a few rods away. I hear the rustle of leaves, sounds of men chiseling stone and driving nails, down the road a boy whistling. And, beyond all these sights and sounds, there are, I know, other sights and other sounds — fields in which birds are singing, the dull roar of great cities, broad rivers, the ocean with the everlasting thunder of its restless waves, and, far beyond, the sun, the moon, other planets, and distant stars.

This is one world. And I belong to it. My body is one of the things that, together, make it up. My body is one of the objects in this room, along with the table, the chairs, and the books.

☙

The world of spirits

And then there is another world. It is made up not of things but of living spirits, of spirits who think and know and feel and love. These spirits — spirits of angels and spirits of men, some of them in bodies like my own and some who have left their bodies — make up a world of spirits. And they belong to one another in that spiritual world. There is "a wonderful order" in which they have their place.

> *Angels and living saints and dead,*
> *But one communion make.*[1]

This spiritual world is what we speak of as "the other world," the "next world." But in using such expressions, we forget that we are in that "other world" more truly than we are in "this," that the "next" world is really the "nearest" world — "Nearer to us than breathing / Closer than hands and feet."

[1] Cf. Isaac Watts, Hymn 152.

Moreover, the spiritual world not only lies behind and penetrates the outer world, but it does, at certain times and places, invade the material world, by manifesting its presence and exercising its power, as, with every daybreak, the light from the sun invades the darkness of this earth. I belong to this spiritual world, for I am a spirit. I can think and know and feel and love. I am one of the spirits that make up the world of spirits.

⌒

God made both worlds

God made both of these worlds. He made all things about me, or the stuff from which they were fashioned by men's hands. He made my body. But God Himself is not one of the objects of this world around me — not even the brightest and most beautiful of them. All the objects of this world might pass away into the nothingness from which they came. But if they were to vanish as "the unsubstantial fabric of a vision," God would not change. What He was before He made all things, that He still is and will be, even though all else should cease to be. "Thou art the same." "From everlasting to everlasting Thou art God."[2]

[2] Cf. Ps. 101:28; 89:2 (RSV = Ps. 102:27; 90:2).

The Work of Prayer

So, again, God made all spirits, of angels and of men. He made me, a spirit. And not only did He make all spirits as He made all things, but He made those spirits for union with Himself, to know Him, fear Him, love Him, work along with Him. In God, who is Spirit, the spirits that He made truly belong to one another. "Hearts can meet only in God."

So the spiritual world has its center and unity in God, far more truly than this earth and the other planets have their center in our sun.

⁓

How we live in each world

To go back to where we started: we belong to these two worlds — the world of bodies or things, and the world of spirits or persons. To live in the world of bodies, I must go out and take from that world what my body needs. I must open my lungs to be filled with air, my mouth to be fed with food, my ears to hear, my eyes to see, my mind to know the things about me.

To live in the world of spirits, I must go out and find in that world what my spirit needs. I must come into communication with God, so that I may know Him, and other spirits in Him. I must try continually to know Him better, so that I may love Him, and others for His sake. I must act out my love to Him by seeking to please Him, to work along with Him, in His plans for me and for His other creatures, for His whole creation.

⌒

Why prayer is necessary

In yet fewer words, if I would live the life of the physical world, I must breathe. If I would live the life of the spiritual world, I must pray. It is not always easy to breathe; there are times when every breath is a struggle, an agony. But if I give up breathing, my body will lose its place in this outward world; that is, it will die.

It is not always easy to pray; there are times when prayer is a struggle, an agony. But if I give up praying, knowing what prayer means, if I give up all that comes to me through prayer, my spirit will lose its place in the spiritual world; that is, it will die, in the sense in which spirits can die.

On the other hand — for still the likeness holds to some definite extent — if I learn to breathe better, if by practice I gain in the habit of "deep-breathing," then my body grows stronger; it has a fuller measure of the life of the material world.

The Work of Prayer

So also, if I learn to pray better, if by practice I come to pray more deeply, with more profound earnestness and trust, then my spirit will grow stronger; it will have a fuller measure of the life of the spiritual world; it will think more clearly, know more fully, feel more keenly, love more intensely; it will come into closer communion with God, the Father of spirits, and with other spirits in Him.

⮑

The spiritual world is supremely important
We belong to two worlds then. Is there any doubt as to which of these two worlds is of supreme importance? The world of things outside of us "passeth away."[3] Scientific men can almost reckon the time at which this earth will turn into a ball of discolored ice, and all life will be extinct. And long, long before that — in fact, within a comparatively few years — each one of us will have drawn the last breath and our place in this world will know us no more. But the world of spirits is the "eternal world." God does not grow old. Although He is "the Ancient of days," yet His "years shall not fail."[4] "God had no beginning and

---

[3] 1 John 2:17.

[4] Dan. 7:9; Ps. 101:28 (RSV = Ps. 102:27).

will have no end." With Him, as St. Augustine[5] says, "there can be neither 'was,' nor 'will be,' but only 'is.' "

The world of spirits who are in union with God is the eternal world. In Him those spirits can have eternal life; they can have that life now, not merely hope to have it by and by. "This is the testimony, that God hath given to us eternal life."[6]

But this eternal life is the life of an immortal spirit — an acting, knowing, loving life. God, who in Spirit, is always acting, knowing, loving. He is pure act. To live by His life we, too, must act and know and love; we must act from Him as our Source, know Him as our Strength, love Him as our Savior. Our Lord said, "My Father *worketh* until now and I *work*."[7] "This is life eternal: to *know* Thee, the only true God."[8] And St. John says, "We have passed from death to life because we *love*."[9]

Here, then, is the inevitable necessity of prayer. For prayer is not only the way to know God; it is the act of

[5] St. Augustine (354-430), Bishop of Hippo.

[6] 1 John 5:11.

[7] John 5:17.

[8] Cf. John 17:3.

[9] 1 John 3:14.

the spirit knowing God and loving Him. Prayer is communion with God; it is entering into fellowship with Him. In its highest and completest exercise, it is sharing His life.

Chapter Two

Understand Who God Is

"Every gross and cruel superstition has this origin
and definition: it springs from ignorance of the Name
of God; it consists in and by that ignorance. . . .
Upon our thoughts of God it will depend,
in one time or another, whether we rise higher
or sink lower as societies and as individuals."

Frederick Denison Maurice

He was a dull, doltish sort of boy, and it seemed rather hopeless to try to rouse him to an interest in anything beyond this outward world, beyond his food and sleep and work. So, when I asked him, "George, do you ever pray?" I was surprised to have him answer, almost with animation, "Yes, I pray." "When do you pray?" I said. "When I have a toothache."

Even such a prayer as this is not to be despised. The crying out for help, under the sharp thrust of pain; the sense of need, and the reaching into the unseen world to find some answer to that need — these might be the starting-point of a true and increasing knowledge of God. But that is just the thing that matters. It might serve as a *beginning*.

Well and good. But what if it became an *end*? What if the boy never went beyond his appeal for help when he had a toothache? What if he never tried to know the One to whom he made appeal? Then he would soon look elsewhere for relief, look to the world about him, and forget that he ever dreamed of any other world than this material sphere. He would find, perhaps, a few drops of laudanum on a piece of cotton wool more efficacious than prayer. Or else, as he experienced the fact that sometimes his toothache stopped, and sometimes it kept on or grew worse, he would have dark and dreadful thoughts about God. He would fancy that God was cruelly teasing him — as he, himself, perhaps, teased the cat or the dog — or that God hated him, and he had a right in return to hate God.

⌒

The word God

In the last chapter, we thought about prayer as the way in which we live and act in the world of spirits, just as breathing is the way in which we live and act in the world of bodies. This is correct if by *prayer* we mean true prayer to the true God. But now we have to face the fact that there may be false gods and wrong prayer. "We must clear our minds [as well as our words] of cant." That is to say, we must ask not only if our words are the faithful expression of our thoughts, but if our thoughts are the faithful reflection of that of which we think.

Perhaps, at the present time, there is no question so necessary to be put to people as: "What do you mean when you use the word God?" For that word may stand for all sorts of notions. And, if we are making some terrible mistake as to what we ought to mean when we say God, we shall make as great a mistake about what we mean when we say *prayer,* and so we shall blunder pitiably when we actually try to pray.

Mistaken ideas of God

Some time ago, a young man wrote me, "I believe in God. I believe He is part of myself." It is quite plain, if that is what he did believe (and I think he was sincere) that, with him, prayer was a monologue, a talking to himself.

It is not uncommon to hear a man say, "I believe in God. I believe He is the Supreme Being." And the very tone of his voice as he makes that statement gives evidence that in his thoughts he is putting God as far from himself and his own affairs as possible. To such a man, prayer becomes as futile as trying to attract the attention of the moon in the midnight heavens.

Then, again, there are those who think of God as, "a big man up in the sky" (as the Mormons frankly say, "God was what we are; we shall be what God is"). Such people will make their prayers in a conversational tone, as though they would instruct God, or offer Him valuable suggestions, or even dictate to Him the course He shall pursue.

To others, still, God is little more than a word written over a door that opens into emptiness, and prayer only a means of cultivating certain sentiments in their own souls.

⌒

Our Father

First of all, then, we must try to have some true knowledge of God, not merely to know *about* Him but to know Him, to know Him as He is, and to know Him in relation to ourselves. "He that cometh to God must believe that He is, and that He is a rewarder of them that diligently seek Him."[10]

This is why we are taught, in the one perfect prayer, to begin by asking, "Our Father . . . hallowed be Thy Name." It might seem as though other needs were more pressing: bread for our bodies, forgiveness for our souls, protection from our enemies. Yet our first great need is

[10] Cf. Heb. 11:6.

that God should make holy to us His Name and His nature, should make us know Him as the Father of our spirits, as our perfect, our heavenly Father: "Our Father who art in Heaven."

⁀

Difficulty of knowing God as our Father

But to know God as our Father, we must know ourselves as His children; and that means that we must think and feel and act as His children, must behave as if He were our Father. And this is where the initial difficulty in prayer arises.

For, in the first place, we have never seen God, as we do see this outward world. And, although we may have felt Him (at least a few times in our lives) the memory of such experience easily grows dim.

Secondly, the aspect of the world about us does not encourage us to believe that God is our "Father" in any sense we naturally give to that word. The cruelty of nature to man, and of man to his fellows, the awful waste of life, the daily tragedies, and the constant thwarting of the highest and the best in human nature make it very difficult to think that He who is behind and above it all is anything like what we instinctively feel a father ought to be.

But, thirdly, to own God as our Father is to confess that we are in a state of entire dependence on Him, that we owe Him gratitude for our every joy, that He seeks and merits our unhesitating obedience, that He claims, and justly claims, our unstinted love. To own this in our daily life is to make the great surrender; it is to live no longer a life centered in self, but a life whose center is God; it is to make of life not a self-interested enterprise, but a loving and self-forgetting response to a divine Father who is infinitely wise, patient, and loving.

The necessity of faith

There is only one way in which this primary difficulty in prayer can be met, and that is by an act of faith. "If thou canst believe."[11] Yet faith is not only necessary for any true relation between man and God; faith is also the only ground for any real friendship between man and man. We can never come to any satisfying knowledge of, or intimacy with, a fellow human being, unless we are ready to make a venture, to trust him, to treat him as though he were worthy of our trust. That alone opens the way for

[11] Mark 9:22.

such a discovery of his character as enables us to prove the wisdom of our faith and trust.

In regard to another human being, we may be mistaken. Yet we must take the risk, or go through life friendless and alone. In regard to God, we cannot be mistaken. He who is infinite in goodness and love can never prove less than we think Him to be. Yet we cannot know this for ourselves save by experience. And, therefore, the first necessity for prayer — that which alone makes true prayer possible — is faith in God. It may be a very dim and hesitating and perplexed faith, but that will be enough if we will act upon it and thereby put ourselves in the way of receiving more of the gift of faith. "Lord, I believe, help Thou mine unbelief."[12]

[12] Cf. Mark 9:23.

Chapter Three

Offer Your Prayer Through Christ

"This one thing is the first and last they learned
of Him: that the personal friendship of Jesus Christ
our Lord was that gift which God was incarnate
to bestow on every man who sought it."

Archbishop Benson

"True prayer is the voice of the child to his Father." That is where we have arrived. But since we must judge of anything by its perfect state, not by any incomplete condition, so to think aright of prayer, we must say that it is "the voice of the perfect Child to the perfect Father." God has always been the perfect Father ("Your Father who is in Heaven is perfect"[13]), but where, in the whole course of this world's experience, shall we find the perfect Child, the perfect Son? Only in One. With bowed heads let us Name Him: Jesus Christ. He is not only a son, He is "*the* Son," "the only-begotten of the Father, full of grace and truth."[14]

God cannot be a sonless Father. And since He is an eternal Father, He has an eternal Son. And inasmuch as God is infinitely perfect, the Son is all that the Father is, united with Him in the most perfect of all unions:

[13] Cf. Matt. 5:48.
[14] John 1:14.

> *Son with the mighty Father One!*
> *The Father wholly in the Son!*

And that eternal and perfect Son has become perfect Man, has lived His life as Man in this very world of ours, in perfect communion with His Father. The communion of the human heart and mind and will of Jesus with His Father was the one perfect prayer. And it is He, Jesus Christ, who makes this prayer possible to us.

⤳

The perfect Father

For first of all, it is He alone who makes God the Father known to us. To the slow-minded Philip, who asked laboringly, "Lord, show us the Father," Jesus said, "He that hath seen me hath seen the Father."[15] Over against all the hideous misery and the more terrible wickedness of the world, stands the Cross of Christ, revealing the infinite tenderness of the Father's love for His disobedient children, for "God was in Christ reconciling the world unto Himself."[16] All the pity and patience, the power and the

[15] Cf. John 14:8, 9.
[16] Cf. 2 Cor. 5:19.

glory that our hearts can long to find in our Father's heart, we behold shown forth to us in Jesus Christ. To His disciples our Lord said, "God so loved the world that He gave His only-begotten Son . . . that the world, through Him, might be saved";[17] "The Father Himself loveth you";[18] "The Father that dwelleth in me doeth the works"; "I am in the Father and the Father in me."[19]

And not only does the Father come to us, revealing His love in Jesus Christ, His Son, but through and in Jesus Christ, we can come to the Father. "No man cometh to the Father but by me."[20] He shows us what is true human *love* to the Father and so what is true human *prayer* to the Father. How much we know, or might know, about the prayer-life of Jesus! "The life of Christ was throughout a life of prayer. Not only did He love to spend many hours in lonely communing with His Father . . . but His whole life was spent in habitual realization of God's presence. The word *Abba* seems to have been constantly on His lips, so that it became one of the watchwords of the Christian

[17] Cf. John 3:16.
[18] John 16:27.
[19] John 14:10.
[20] John 14:6.

community, the sound of which those who had been with Jesus never forgot."

⤙

Perfect prayer

Jesus shows us what true prayer is, what it meant to Him, the perfect Son, to speak to His Father; how He, while here on earth, was also continually in the spiritual world ("the Son of Man who is in Heaven"[21]). And then, as we watch Him, the desire springs up in our hearts to do what He is doing. So it was with the first disciples. "And it came to pass, that as He was praying in a certain place, when He ceased, one of His disciples said unto Him, 'Lord, teach us to pray.' "[22] And then He gave them, and gives us, the Our Father, the pattern and summing up of all prayer.

⤙

The Our Father

The first word in that prayer, in the Greek, Latin, German, and other languages, although not in English, is

[21] John 3:13.
[22] Luke 11:1.

Father. Our Lord utters the word that we may say it after Him and may try to give to it for ourselves something of what it meant to Him. So we exercise the privilege of our sonship, being sons of God.

The second word is *our.* That word, if we live up to its significance, rescues our prayer from all selfishness. For the *our,* or *of us,* takes in every soul in the world; in some sense it takes in all creation. So we do not pray alone. We are in fellowship with all God's creatures. So we recognize every man and woman as a brother or a sister, and ask for each and all the very same that we ask for ourselves.

The next four words, "Who art in Heaven," take us out of the prison-house of outward things and make us free for the "other world," the world of spiritual life. "In entering the world of prayer, we enter the world of reality." It is from that vantage-ground that we can rightly ask for the supply of all our needs, of body, mind, or soul.

Then follow the seven great petitions. The word common to the first three is *Thy:* "Thy Name," "Thy kingdom," "Thy will," taking us back to the first word of the prayer, *Father.* The word common to the last four petitions is *us:* "Give us," "Forgive us," "Lead us not," "Deliver us," which takes us back to the second word of the whole prayer, *our.*

The Work of Prayer

It will help very much, if occasionally, we say the Our Father clause by clause, as though hearing the voice of Jesus saying the words, trying to grasp more and more of the meaning that He gives to the words; confident that, although the words have been spoken so many million times, and by the greatest saints of the Church, their whole meaning has never yet been compassed in this world.

☙

Prayer in Jesus

But this is not all. It is not enough that our Lord should show us in His own life what true prayer is. Nor is it enough that He should teach us in His own patient and loving fashion how we are to pray, saying for us the very words that we may use, so that we may experience "the sense of dependence upon God and the way to have speech with Him." All that, although in far inferior degree, any wise and holy man might do for us. But there is that which we need and which only He who is the God-Man can do on our behalf.

We belong to a race that has revolted from God, and we have forfeited our place as children of the Father. We need to be recovered to our true sonship, to be restored to our home. And this is what Jesus does for us, what none other but He could do. He takes us up into Himself, so that in our baptism we are born again and are identified with Him. He took our nature so that we might partake with Him of the divine nature.[23] As St. Augustine says, "The Son of God became the Son of Man, that the sons of men might become sons of God." In Him our whole nature is redeemed and renewed, and His manhood becomes a transforming principle in us.

We are members of the Body of Christ, and we act in Him, our Head. Because He is the perfect Son, and we are in Him, therefore we have received the adoption of sons and are in true filial relation to the Father. It is not only that we say, "Our Father" *after* Him; we say it *in* Him — nay, He says it in us. The voice of the well-beloved sounds in every true Christian prayer, and we are accepted in Him.

And being thus taken up into Him, we can plead all that He is and all that He has done. We lift up the Cross before the face of our Father and ask to be heard because of the Sacrifice offered there; because of the unmerited but willing endurance by our Lord of all suffering and of

[23] Cf. 2 Pet. 1:4.

death itself; because of the victory of the Crucified over all the foes that would hold us back from God.

> *Look, Father, look on His anointed Face*
> *And only look on us as found in Him;*
> *Look not on our misusings of Thy grace,*
> *Our prayer so languid, and our faith so dim:*
> *For lo! between our sins and their reward*
> *We set the Passion of Thy Son, our Lord.*[24]

[24] William Bright, "And Now, O Father, Mindful of the Love," stanza 2.

Chapter Four

Let the Holy Spirit Guide Your Prayer

"We do not pray to change the divine scheme,
but to ask those things which God has decreed
to be brought about in response to our prayers."

St. Thomas Aquinas

A picture used to hang in my mother's chamber during the later years of her life. It had little artistic merit, but the sentiment that produced it seemed genuine and sincere. The picture portrayed a simple bedroom, in an old-fashioned farmhouse, with bare floor and sloping ceiling. Through a dormer window shone the warm glow of a summer sunset. Within, the darkness was already gathering in the corners of the room, but the wide bedstead was still in light. Curled on the bed was a black kitten asleep, or purring softly. And, kneeling at the foot of the bed, her arms folded on the worn quilt, her face hidden on her arms, was a little girl, in long white shift, saying her night prayers.

Such a scene brings different suggestions to different minds. Among them is the sense of contrast between the two worlds described in the first chapter of this book. One of these is the world of outward things, things that can be seen and heard and handled. The other is the spiritual world of personal thought and will and action.

The Work of Prayer

⌒

Prayer unites the two worlds

As an event in this material world, in the unfolding of the earth's physical history, the little child at her prayers, alone in the quiet room, is of utter insignificance, scarcely more important than the chirp of the August cricket in the wet grass outside, or the twinkle of the evening star, shining clearer as the sunset fades.

But if we open our minds to the spiritual world, what tremendous personal forces meet in the utterance of that little heart. For, to render possible that child's prayer, the infinite and eternal God — Father, Son, and Holy Spirit — must be acting in the fullness of His love and power, at this very point of time and space, at this evening hour, in this darkening room.

⌒

What true prayer involves

That Christian child could not say one word of true and acceptable prayer unless God the Father had willed that she should speak to Him; unless God the Son had become Man, died, rose again, and was pleading His Passion in mighty intercession so that she might come to the Father in Him; and unless God the Holy Spirit was giving her the words to speak and taking His place in her heart to say the words with her. "And when that cry goes up before the Throne, it will be heard and remembered because the Holy Spirit prepared and sent it, the Son perfected it, the Father received it. Therefore, every child's lispings of prayer enfold all the mysteries of the Eternal Trinity."

☞

Prayer does not originate with us

This is only what St. Paul tells all Christians, old or young, when he says that God has "sent the Spirit of His Son into your hearts, crying: Abba, Father,"[25] and that they all, through Jesus Christ who, "reconciled them unto God by His Cross, [have] access by one Spirit unto the Father,"[26] and that no one can say, "Lord Jesus, but by the Holy Spirit."[27]

It is of this that we now need to think. The prayers that I say, if they are true Christian prayers, do not begin with me. I do not originate them, although they express my deepest longings, my truest self. These prayers come to me

[25] Gal. 4:6.
[26] Cf. Rom. 5:10; Eph. 2:18.
[27] Cf. 1 Cor. 12:3.

from God the Holy Spirit. He breathes into me, by the *inspiration* of His love, the "holy desires," which then, by His help, I breathe out, in *aspiration* to God. And, by that same Spirit, these desires are carried up to the Father's loving heart and accepted through the mediation of His well-beloved Son.

Thus is met the second difficulty in the life of prayer. We say that true prayer requires a true knowledge of God, such as results from *faith* in Him as He made Himself known to us. But, then, further the question comes: "Are the praises that I try to offer to God, or the petitions I present, really such as God can accept? Are they not too cold and weak to win His attention and approval?"

And there is only one way in which this second difficulty in the life of prayer can be met. That is by an act of *hope*. Not hope in ourselves, but hope in the purpose and power of the Holy Spirit to "pray the prayer within us that to Heaven shall rise," to "sing the song that angels sing above the skies."

⌐

Familiar difficulties in prayer

Let us go into this matter somewhat more fully. No complaints are more familiar to those who try to help souls than: "I can't pray"; "I can't keep my thoughts from wandering"; "I can't make myself feel earnest or devout"; "It makes me cross to say my prayers. I am sure it is no use to pray when I feel like that. It is only mocking God."

Now these complaints come almost always from a mistake about prayer of which we must be rid if we wish to pray aright. The mistake is to think that if I keep my mind steadily fixed on what I am praying about, and if my heart is stirred with devotional feeling, then my prayer will be pleasing to God. But that, on the other hand, if my mind is distracted and confused, and my emotions are dull or dead, then my prayer will fall back, unable to rise to God, like a bird with a broken wing. In other words that, although I must make my prayer "through Jesus Christ our Lord," yet the starting-point of the prayer is in myself, and its effectiveness is dependent upon the force and intensity that I myself give to it.

This view of prayer sounds reasonable and is not so easily detected, since a half-truth is often more dangerous than open error. But plausible as it may be, its effect is strangely disheartening. For it implies that prayer is necessary if we are to take and keep our place in the spiritual world, but that we must, by some effort of our own, take and keep our place in the spiritual world in order to pray;

that to know and love God we must pray to Him, but that God will receive our prayer according to our natural ability to know and love Him; that prayer is the way to become saints, but that we must be saints in order to pray, or, at least, to pray with confidence in the result.

~

Prayer is God's gift

Where is the flaw in this apparent deadlock? It lies in forgetting that prayer itself, as well as the answer to prayer, is a *gift* bestowed upon us, not because we *deserve* it, but because we *need* it. And the worth of prayer comes not from what we think, or from what we feel, but from what the Holy Spirit does. By my prayer I do not move God to come to me, but God moves me to come to Him.

The whole matter can be stated in a few words. There are certain things that God wants to give me, or wants to enable me to do toward Him. So, at the proper time He sends His Holy Spirit to stir in me the desire for that which He has made ready for me to have or to do. If I welcome this desire, the Holy Spirit within my soul uses its powers — mind, affection, will — to turn the desire into words and to make of the words a prayer to God. The prayer-value depends not upon the human spirit but upon the divine Spirit. "The prayer, therefore, is part of the gift. It is the channel which God Himself opens in a man's heart through which He may pour the blessing He purposes to bestow." "Our prayers are not right prayers if they are not the work of the divine Spirit within us, wanting what God wants."

~

Prayer is our work

Does this mean that I am dispensed from making any effort, that I can take my ease because Another speaks through me? No, indeed. While prayer is on God's part a gift, it must on my part, with His help, be a labor and a struggle: a labor in which all my faculties are employed; a struggle against my spiritual foes who would stifle the "voice of my cry." I must do my best to resist distractions, to mean the words I say, to desire what God put into my heart to ask from Him. It is only as I do my best that I show that I really want the Holy Spirit to pray within me, that I open my heart to receive His gift of prayer.

"The effectual fervent prayer of a righteous man availeth much,"[28] but not as though the righteousness were the

[28] Cf. James 5:16.

man's own personal possession. The "righteous man" is one who is learning more and more his own weakness, and is turning more and more from himself to God, so that God is more and more free to carry out His will in him. Yet this very surrender is the man's own development in righteousness in the way of effective prayer. Man is never more truly himself than when he is working along with God, and he is never more free than when the Holy Spirit is inspiring him so to work. Yet in this cooperation with God, the one essential thing is that man shall be conscious that he is wholly dependent upon Him. And, with a creature as self-assertive as man, it is often the very dullness and distraction of his mind, the very lumpishness and reluctance of his will, the very coldness and deadness of his feelings that fling him back upon the Holy Spirit to do for him and in him and through him that which he cannot do for himself.

> For Thou art oft most present, Lord,
> In weak, distracted prayer;
> A sinner out of heart with self
> Most often finds Thee there.
>
> For prayer that humbles sets the soul
> From all delusion free,

And teaches it how utterly,
Dear Lord, it hangs on Thee.

Thrice blessed by the darkness, then,
This deep in which I lie;
And blessed be all things that teach
God's dear supremacy.

❧

A word of encouragement

So the very best and loudest prayer in the ear of God may come from a soul that feels itself bereft of His light and love, and yet, for that very reason, longs all the more yearningly to be able to speak to Him. Let such a soul abandon itself to its mighty Comrade and Friend, the Holy Spirit. If it find no other words, let it say, "Lord, I believe; help Thou mine unbelief."[29] "Lord, take my soul, for I cannot make it Thine, and keep it, for I cannot keep it Thine." Or if its case seems still more desperate, let it cry with Jesus on His Cross, "My God, my God, why hast Thou forsaken me?"[30]

[29] Cf. Mark 9:23.
[30] Matt. 27:46.

Chapter Five

Fit Prayer into Your Day

"Prayer is possible at any time and at all occupations,
but the man who prays when he is cleaning his
boots is most likely to be the man who
has set apart time to keep up the habit."

John Neville Figgis

Is it good to have a rule as to our prayers, to establish a habit as to what we shall say to God and when we shall say it?

It is not uncommon to meet with a definite objection to any set time or forms for devotion. "Is it not very mechanical," it is asked, "to say prayers according to a fixed rule? Ought not prayer to be spontaneous and free? Do not prayers thus said become perforce unreal or superstitious?"

It would be foolish to ignore the dangers we meet in taking up a rule as to our prayers. It is true that we may come to say them thoughtlessly. We may ease our conscience by merely saying them. "By rule" may come to be "by rote."

On the other hand, if we have no order or method for our devotions, and pray only when we feel like it, there is at least an equal danger that we shall grow less and less disposed to prayer, and that infrequency will end in neglect. What we may do at any time is often what we actually do at no time.

How shall we solve this dilemma? We must find out what kind of prayer is most to the honor of God, and most needful for ourselves; what is most pleasing to Him, and most profitable — not most pleasant — for us.

⁀

A rule of prayer honors God

In the last chapter, we saw that what counts with God is the movement of our wills toward Him, the purpose that lies behind our acts, what we *mean*, not what we *feel*. We could not pray at all unless we had the will to pray. It is just the offering of our wills that opens the way for the Holy Spirit to plead within us.

Now, to adopt a definite rule for prayers is to determine that we will speak to God, not only *now* and *here*, but that we will go on speaking to Him, regularly, no matter what our mood may be — even when we are reluctant to make the effort. A rule of prayer gives a pledge that we mean to persevere in prayer, and to be "faithful unto death."[31]

It is easy to see that, in binding ourselves by such a rule, we are making a far more comprehensive act of will than when we pray by some sudden impulse, which, however strong at the moment, passes away, and leaves no abiding purpose whereby we give to God not only the

---

[31] Apoc. 2:10 (RSV = Rev. 2:10).

present but the future. The more we surrender our
selves, what we are and what we are to be, in response to
the eternal love of God, the better is the prayer we make
to Him.

&

A rule of prayer helps us

And, then, most of us need just the kind of stimulus
that a rule of prayer supplies. Difficulties and hindrances
in prayer must be faced. At times we shall be dull and dry,
and prayer will bring no refreshment or relief. Such trials
may be the result of past unfaithfulness on our part, or,
again, they may rise from no fault of our own.

"My son, if thou come to serve the Lord, prepare thy
soul for temptation."[32] Prayer is not only communion with
God. It is also a struggle with our spiritual foes. Both flesh
and spirit flag in that encounter. No doubt "Satan trem-
bles when he sees / The weakest saint upon his knees."[33]
But that does not prevent him from doing his utmost to
defeat the effort of the humble saint, to drug his senses,
distract his mind, perplex his soul, discourage his spirit.

[32] Cf. Ecclus. 2:1 (RSV = Sir 2:1).
[33] William Cowper, "Exhortation to Prayer."

In such conflicts, a well-ordered rule is of priceless worth, provided we look, not to ourselves, but to God for strength to keep it, provided we see in the rule the will of God for us and fling ourselves upon His sustaining power. By means of the rule, God tides us over the seasons of depression and assault.

> *For this the vow was spoken*
> *That the low days might be true.*

Nor does a rule of prayer render us less prompt to speak to God when the impulse stirs within us. Regularity in prayer develops the prayer-attitude of dependence and trust, so that we can, at last, as the apostle bids us, "pray without ceasing."[34] "Times, places, and postures in prayer are to be used, not until we come to be independent of them but until we come to universalize them, making all life one sacrament."

How to frame a rule of prayer

Let us essay the drawing up of a rule of prayer. It would, of course, form a large part of any rule of *life*, for such a

[34] 1 Thess. 5:17.

rule is an ordering of our daily actions and interests in reference to God as their true end, and among all the things we do or say, prayer should have the central and fundamental place. If our prayer is right, then all else will tend to be right. St. Teresa[35] says that no one can pray a quarter of an hour a day and be lost; she means earnest and sincere prayers, the heart of which is "Thy will be done."

⌒

Each day is a life in little

In drawing up a rule of prayer, we naturally begin with the arrangement of our daily devotions. The aim in putting in order the prayers we offer each day should be that in them we may do the most for God, for others, and for ourselves. This is in accordance with a right estimate of what each day should mean to us.

A Latin proverb bids us, "Treat each day as a life." For every day is a sort of miniature of our whole earthly existence. We come out of the unconsciousness of sleep in the morning, as though we were beginning life afresh. We pass

[35] Likely St. Teresa of Avila (1515-1582), Spanish Carmelite nun, mystic, and Doctor.

into the unconsciousness of sleep at night, as though life in this world were over.

Now, there are two times when we are told it would be a sin not to pray. One of these is when, as little children, we first come to a knowledge of God and realize that to Him, as our Father, we owe our very being. The other time is when we come to die and know that, in a little while, we are to meet Him as our Judge, in the particular judgment. There is, therefore, very strong reason for beginning and ending each day with prayer, for making prayer "the key of the morning and the bolt of the night."

Our morning recollection

How shall we direct our morning prayers? The presence of God should be our first thought on waking, as though His look and voice and touch had aroused us. It should become as natural to us on waking to whisper, "God" or "Jesus" as it is for the little child, disturbed in sleep, to murmur, "Mother."

This instinctive looking up to God with implicit adoration of His majesty and love for His goodness is what is called *recollection*. It is the most universal form of prayer, the prayer we can practice at all times and places, the prayer of which St. Paul was thinking when he wrote to his disciples in Macedonia, "Pray without ceasing." Recollection has many degrees of intensity, but in some degree it is always possible.

☞

Recollection of others and of God

We can recollect the presence of other persons when we are engaged in the most engrossing occupation. This is a singular psychological fact, but it is one with which we are perfectly familiar. There is hardly any intellectual effort more absorbing than to speak extemporaneously before a great audience on some momentous occasion. Yet in the midst of the most impassioned appeal, the speaker is keenly conscious of those whom he is addressing, of various individuals in the audience, of their attitude toward him and toward what he is saying, of the reaction he is producing in their minds. All this does not hinder his utterance; on the contrary, it stirs his mental powers to the very utmost effort of which they are capable.

If that is true of our recollection of other human beings like ourselves, it must be not less but more true of recollection of the presence of God. Just as we may work with utmost diligence, hour after hour, in a room where another person is present, tinglingly alive at every instant to that other personality, so we may be ever conscious of God, doing all as "in our great Taskmaster's eye,"[36] offering up all we do as done for Him. "Whether you eat or drink or whatsoever you do, do all to the glory of God."[37]

◦

Recollection conscious and unconscious

Yet not only may recollection be an act of which we are fully conscious. It may go on in the subconsciousness, as in the hours of rest at night. "I sleep, but my heart waketh," says the bride in the Canticle.[38] When we remember that God is more intimately present to our souls than life is to our bodies, we shall see that the moment of waking is not the passing of the spirit from a realm where God is not to a world in which He is, but rather from a condition in which we know God instinctively and immediately to one in which we must seek Him behind the veil of outward things. This may be the explanation of an experience that some at least who read this have known,

---

[36] Cf. John Milton, "How Soon Hath Time," line 14.

[37] 1 Cor. 10:31.

[38] Cf. Cant. 5:2 (RSV = Song of Sol. 5:2).

when, on waking, we seem to be aware of a presence that has but just removed itself from us, as though, had we but wakened a moment sooner, we would have seen Him standing beside us.

At any rate, it is our privilege, by making the thought of God fill the last moment of consciousness as we fall asleep, to find the moment of waking one of loving recollection of Him, a recollection that we must try to renew all day long, as the clock strikes, or the bell rings, or as we catch sight of some object like the crucifix that recalls the thought of God, until there are fewer and fewer moments that are not blessed by a recognition of His never-ceasing care and love.

Chapter 6

Begin Your Day with Prayer

"I know not which is the greater wonder,
either that prayer, which is a duty so easy and facile,
so ready and adapted to the powers and skill and
opportunities of every man, should have so great
effects, and be productive of such mighty blessings;
or that we should be so unwilling to use so easy
an instrument of procuring so much good."

Jeremy Taylor

"Charlie, why do you say your prayers at night, but not in the morning?" "Why, at night I want God to take care of me, but in the daytime I can take care of myself." Most of the excuses people give for not beginning the day with prayer are about as sensible as this.

If there is any truth in the adage "Well begun is half done," it must apply in a unique way to the conduct of each day of our life, that particular section of our work in this world that is bounded by our waking in the morning and our falling asleep at night. And can any day be said to be "well begun" if we have entered upon it without reference to God, without taking Him into account?

If, as was urged in the last chapter, we form the habit of filling the first moment of waking with an adoring thought of God, then we shall want at once to act toward Him. The recollection of which we have been thinking is not merely an intellectual reminiscence, as when we recall some object or persons in the outward world. It must mean a movement not only of the mind but of the heart and the will. The mother who wakes at night and recalls her little child not only *thinks* of him, but *loves* him and *acts* as she reaches her hand out to make sure he is safe beside her, to draw the coverlet more snugly about the sleeping form.

⁀

The three morning prayers

With what acts, then, should we accompany our waking recollection of God? There are three acts that seem essential to a true response to Him who has been watching over us while we slumbered, who raises us up for another day of service to Him, without whom we can accomplish nothing really good in the hours that lie before us. These acts may be named adoration, dedication, and supplication. About each of them there is much to be said.

⁀

Adoration

First, we should praise God. This is the primal debt that every creature owes to the Creator. So the angels, as they sprang into being, broke into a torrent of praise to God. The holy angels carry on that praise ceaselessly forever.

We are to join them every morning. Creation began with a burst of praise; so should each day of our created life.

Praise to God on the part of an intelligent creature is an acknowledgment of His infinite perfection, with a heartfelt admiration and *adoration* of His unspeakable praiseworthiness.

> *My God, how wonderful Thou art,*
> *Thy majesty how bright.*
> *How beautiful Thy mercy-seat,*
> *In depths of burning light.*
>
> *How wonderful, how beautiful*
> *The sight of Thee must be,*
> *Thine endless wisdom, boundless power,*
> *And awful purity.*

Of all the many forms of prayer, there is none that calls for more care and faithfulness than this adoration or praise. It is in worship and adoration that we are definitely practicing for the endless *Alleluia* of the heavenly courts. Other modes of address to almighty God will pass away, but the citizens on high will praise God forever and ever.

And it is in adoration and praise that we escape from the last entanglements of self-centeredness and self-love.

Work of Prayer

Vocal prayer rises to its loftiest climax in the words of our eucharistic worship, "We give thanks to Thee for Thy great glory." There self is forgotten. There we escape from self "in adoration, self-surrender, and blessing; in the awe and joy of welcoming the presence of the Eternal Beauty, the Eternal Sanctity, and the Eternal Love, the Sacrifice and Reconciliation of the world."

The supreme provision in this world of an adoration that at the same time humbles us to the dust and exalts us to Heaven is afforded us in the holy Mass, where our great High Priest offers Himself to His Father as our Sacrifice of praise and thanksgiving, and gathers up the worship of earth and Heaven.

Dedication

The second act we should make at the beginning of the day is that of dedicating ourselves afresh to God, to be His alone, to be used by Him as He sees best, in the carrying out of His holy and blessed will. All that we are is His gift to be restored to Him. He created us for Himself, so that we might find our joy in Him. We are to be prepared, at His call, to meet the joys and sorrows, pains or pleasures that the day may bring.

A saintly spirit has expressed this dedication of self in words that we may aspire to make our own:

> O Adonai, O Ruler of Israel, Thou that guidest Joseph like a flock, O Emmanuel, O Sapientia, I give myself to Thee. I trust Thee wholly. Thou art wiser than I — more loving to me than I myself. Deign to fulfill Thy high purposes in me, whatsoever they be; work in and through me. I am born to serve Thee, to be Thine, to be Thy instrument. Let me be Thy blind instrument. I ask not to see, I ask not to know, I ask simply to be used.

Such an act of dedication sets a keynote for the whole day for all that we may undertake, for the tasks that we have done a thousand times before and for the adventure upon new and untried paths. We are to renew this offering of ourselves more and more often, until we become "conscious acts of dedication, giving ourselves to God with every breath we draw," following "the Lamb whithersoever He goeth."[39] The Church calls upon us thus to offer ourselves at every Eucharist: "Here we offer and present unto Thee, O Lord, ourselves, our souls and bodies, to be a

[39] Apoc. 14:4 (RSV = Rev. 14:4).

reasonable, holy, and living sacrifice unto Thee," and each Eucharist should set before us the ideal of our every action. We are "to worship God in everything we do," and our worship must be a sacrifice of self, in union with the "tremendous Sacrifice" pleaded every morning on the altars of the Church.

⌇

Supplication

It is not necessary to say to those who have read this chapter thus far that prayer does not mean only asking God to give us things. That is the notion of it in the minds of worldly and unspiritual people. They think of it as a sort of device whereby we may hope to obtain from God what we want, even if He is not much disposed that we should have it. It is strange and sad enough that persons who have had a Christian upbringing should so think of prayer. For this, as was shown in the fourth chapter, quite reverses the whole process of prayer, putting ourselves first, rather than God, and seeking not to bring our will to Him, but to bend His will to ours.

What we must try to realize is that the background of all supplication, of all asking from God, is the prayer of adoration and of dedication. The pleading of the Holy

Eucharist by a faithful communicant is the most powerful of all petitions that go up to the God who answers prayer. It is in our Communion that we shall fully learn that God, who is the Infinite Love, desires our true happiness infinitely more than we can wish for it, and we must be sure that nothing could possibly be better for us than that the primary will of God for us should be carried out, that the heart of every petition we make to God is, "Not my will but Thine be done."[40] The condition of any true supplication to God is clearly given by St. John: "Whatsoever we ask, we receive of Him, because we keep His commandments, and do those things that are pleasing in His sight." "And this is the confidence that we have in Him: that, if we ask anything *according to His will*, He heareth us."[41]

People sometimes ask querulously, "If it is God's will that I should have all that I need, all that is good for me, why must I ask Him for it?" The answer is very simple: Because there are things that God wills that I shall have, if I have them at all, in answer to my prayers. God made me for Himself. He gives me many things without my asking for them. I did not ask that the sun should rise this

[40] Luke 22:42.
[41] Cf. 1 John 3:22; 5:14.

morning, or that the mail should arrive. But there are things that I must ask for. God made me for Himself; the whole universe without Him would be nothing to me. I cannot have God, save as I know Him and love Him. If God were to give me everything I need without my asking Him for anything, I might easily forget Him. Of the wicked it is said, "He gave them their desire and sent leanness withal into their soul."[42]

Moreover, since God has made me in His own image, and calls me to be like Him, I cannot have what I need most unless by my own will I choose Him, and cry to Him for light whereby to know Him, and love whereby to be united to Him. If I do not pray, mine will be the doom: "You have not, because you ask not."[43]

Therefore I fall to prayer for what I need, and above all for grace to make all the experiences of this day an occasion for knowing God better and for loving Him more.

So, we should own our weakness and ask God to guard and guide, to support and strengthen us. So only can we, with true Christian courage, go forth day by day into this terrible world.

[42] Ps. 105:15 (RSV = 106:15).
[43] James 4:2.

A prayer on rising

It has taken us some time to consider the three acts of adoration, dedication, and supplication. But those acts can be made in the saying of a very brief form of words. Such a form is given here to be said, if possible, on one's knees, immediately upon rising, after making the Sign of the Cross.

> *I praise my God this day;*
> *I give myself to God this day;*
> *I ask God to help me this day.*

The origin of this prayer may be of interest. Thirty-odd years ago, when working in the New York tenements, I was speaking to one of my boys about his morning prayers. He was a little fellow, much underweight for his age, but he was already at work in one of the big factories. He told me quite frankly that he was so tired every morning that his mother had to pull him out of bed and how, after gulping a cup of hot coffee, he had to run to the factory. He didn't see where he could get in his morning prayer. I asked him up how many flights he lived — most of our people seemed to live on the top floor. He said he was up three flights. "Then," I said, "I will give you a prayer to say on each flight, and they will all be said before you get out on the street." I found that he used the prayers I gave him. Since then I have taught these prayers to some thousands of children.

Other morning devotions

Few of those who read this are so hard pressed for time as the little boy of whom I just made mention. They ought certainly to spend some time in prayer before leaving their rooms. The expressions "spend some time in prayer" is used purposely, for many persons would find that they can pray with much less distraction if they keep a clock or a watch in sight and are determined to give a full five or ten minutes to real communication with God, instead of aiming to repeat a certain number of prayers and so laying themselves open to the temptation to hurry through them and save time. "Hurry is the ruin of devotion." But while one can hurry the saying of a form of words, one cannot hasten the passage of time.

Suppose you have said the prayer just given immediately on rising. During your ablutions, you might repeat the vows of your Baptism and perhaps say from memory a psalm. While dressing, you could make the "examination of forethought," looking forward to the day and preparing yourself to meet with some special temptation to ill-temper, discouragement, or tardiness. Then, when you are ready to leave your room, you could read five verses in the Bible — from the Gospels or the Psalms — and then kneel and say the following acts of faith, hope, and love.

> My God, I believe in Thee, and all that
> Thy Church doth teach, because Thou
> hast said it, and Thy word is true.
>
> My God, I hope in Thee for grace
> and for glory, because of Thy mercy,
> Thy promises, and Thy power.
>
> My God, I love Thee, and for Thy sake
> I desire to love my neighbor as myself.

Then you could say the *Kyrie*,[44] the Our Father, and some prayer or prayers in your own words, concluding by standing and saying the Creed as a battle cry before going out to the day's conflict.

---

[44] See "Prayers for Every Day," which follows the last chapter, for the words to this and other prayers.

The Work of Prayer

Everyone should make his own book of private devotions, writing out new prayers and changing them from time to time, and having a list of days on which he wishes to make special devotions.

All this could be done, without haste and with real attention, in less than five minutes. The Our Father by itself takes less than half a minute, said with full attention. And yet people assert that they have no time to say their morning prayers!

Chapter Seven

Devote Time to Mental Prayer

"A great master of the spiritual life said
'I have learned to meditate by taking a verse
of the Gospel, or a truth of the Faith,
and thinking it over with God.' "

Canon Liddon

Any description of prayer, and of a rule of prayer, would be very incomplete if it did not include the practice of meditation, or mental prayer. The difficulty at this point is not that so little has been said and written about meditation, but that so much has been said and written about it that people have taken fright and imagined that it must be a very elaborate and difficult affair, requiring vigorous intellectual effort such as is hardly possible, save for trained minds. As a matter of fact, while there are forms of meditation that are suited to saints and philosophers, there are also forms that are among the simplest devotional exercises and that require less mental effort than adding up a column of figures.

Meditation is not a strain

Indeed, many people stumble at meditation not because they do not try hard enough, but because they try too hard — that is to say, with too much straining of mind and nerves, too much activity of the human spirit. Meditation is a very quiet attitude of the heart, waiting quite simply and patiently for God to say to it what He will. As the old peasant pointing to the tabernacle said to the Curé d'Ars,[45] "I look at Him, and He looks at me." The motto for meditation is "My soul waiteth in stillness upon God,"[46] or "I will hearken what the Lord God will say concerning me."[47] "Speak, Lord, for Thy servant heareth."[48]

An illustration from daily life

Let me take an illustration from our experience of human relations. Here is a youth starting out in life, going to college, or leaving home to take a position. He has just received a letter from an older friend, a former teacher perhaps, or a priest who has known him since childhood. The youth is conscious of the interest his friend takes in him;

---

[45] Curé of Ars (1786-1859), St. John Vianney: patron saint of parish priests.

[46] Cf. Ps. 61:6 (RSV = Ps. 62:5).

[47] Ps. 84:9 (RSV = Ps. 85:8).

[48] 1 Kings 3:10 (RSV = 1 Sam. 3:10).

he is convinced of his friend's good judgment and of his high standards of life and conduct. He feels that his friend understands him better than he does himself and that a much longer and larger experience of life enables his friend to appreciate what lies before him much better than he can.

So the youth is not content to read his friend's letter hurriedly through and then throw it aside. On the contrary, he keeps it by him, and, as occasion offers, in some pause of his work, or when walking to and fro on his accustomed beat, he takes the letter out and studies it, turning the sentences over and over in his mind, and trying to gather from them all that his friend sought to convey to him through them.

That is meditation, when the Friend is God, and the letter is the record of His revelation of Himself, brought to its fullness in the life and death and Resurrection of Jesus Christ.

༄

Directions for meditation

A meditation could be made at any time of the day, except that it had better not be made just before retiring for the night. No particular place or posture is necessary, but it is good to fix upon a certain definite length of time — ten minutes at first — and to choose a time and place in which you will not be overcome by sleepiness. As suggested above, a meditation could be made when walking from place to place outdoors.

I remember as a boy how my mother, when she came in from doing her marketing, or about that time if she did not go out, used to sit down in her room with her devotional books for half an hour, and during this time, it was not the thing for us children to interrupt her. I doubt if she thought of herself as "making a meditation," but I am quite sure that she was in personal converse with Almighty God.

The meditation should be begun and ended with direct prayer to God and, as just suggested, should tend to become more and more a colloquy with Him. The pattern for meditation should be formed in the intimate conversations that the disciples held with Jesus, when He was visibly with them, when they sat with Him in the boat on the Sea of Galilee, or when He talked with them by the way.

As prayer should result in some practical doing of God's will, so at the end of the meditation, it is good to form some resolution to be carried out later in the day, something very simple and explicit.

Chapter Eight

Pray Throughout the Day

"Forenoon and afternoon and night,
Forenoon and afternoon and night,
Forenoon and — what? No more?
Yea, that is life. But make that forenoon sublime,
That afternoon a psalm, that night a prayer,
And time is conquered and thy crown is won."

Edward Rowland Sill

A certain number of people will find the noon hour a suitable time for making a meditation. Whether they do so or not, it is certainly well to mark the passing of the sun over the meridian by some definite brief prayer.

During the Great War, I was in the city of Poughkeepsie about the middle of an ordinary weekday. As the city clock struck twelve, I suddenly saw the policeman who directs traffic at Main and Market streets standing at attention. Glancing about, I saw others here and there halting their steps and standing silent. On inquiring, I was told that an order had been issued that half a minute should be given at noon daily on behalf of the men at the front.

I do not know how far this custom was followed in other places or how long this order was in force, but it is certain that every noon thousands of prayers go up to God and that ours should have a place among them.

The devotion that more than any other has gradually associated itself with noon, as well as early in the morning and toward evening, is the *Angelus*.[49] The noon *Angelus* is a memorial of the Passion as that in the morning is of the Resurrection and that in the evening of the Incarnation. The devotion is called the *Angelus* because that is the first word in the Latin: *Angelus Domini nuntiavit Mariae* ("The Angel of the Lord declared unto Mary"). Of course, any other prayers may be used, and those that refer to our Lord's death on the Cross are peculiarly appropriate; for example, the *Salvator Mundi*:

> *O Savior of the world, who by*
> *Thy Cross and Precious Blood*
> *hast redeemed us,*
> *save us, and help us, we humbly*
> *beseech Thee, O Lord.*

Memory of the Passion

It is plainly the desire of the Church that we should "always remember the exceeding great love of our Master, and only Savior, Jesus Christ . . . dying for us, and the innumerable benefits which by His precious blood-shedding

---

[49] See "Prayers for Every Day," following the last chapter.

He hath obtained for us."[50] It was to this end that our Lord instituted the Holy Mass. "Do this for my memorial."[51] "As often as you eat this bread and drink this cup, you show the Lord's death till He come."[52] "O Sacred Banquet wherein . . . the memory of His Passion is renewed."

But there are many other means whereby the atoning death of our Lord is brought before us. There is the cross set up, shining on the altar or on the spire of the church, or hung on the wall of our room. There is the Friday abstinence,[53] marking the day on which He died. There is the Sign of the Cross, which we make many times a day, from forehead to breast, from left to right. There are pictures and hymns and emblems that recall the incidents of the Passion.

By all these and by many other means, the Church strives to keep fresh in our minds the mystery of Divine Love sacrificing itself for a guilty world to bring healing and peace to men.

[50] *Book of Common Prayer*.

[51] Cf. Luke 22:19.

[52] Cf. 1 Cor. 11:26.

[53] The Catholic observance of abstaining from eating meat on Fridays is now required only on Ash Wednesday and on Fridays during Lent.

The Work of Prayer

֍

Acted prayer

Before we pass from noon prayer to night prayers, it may be of service to point out a form of prayer somewhat more energetic than recollection, and yet consistent with keen attention to external effort, especially manual effort and physical exertion.

There are many people nowadays who are hurried along in the rush of social life, of competitive industry, who have a painful sense of a duel between work and prayer. The two operations seem to them mutually exclusive, yet they are convinced that both are necessary. They must work. They must also pray. But how are they to proportion these expenditures of vital force, to adjust their claims? When such people are working, often most unselfishly for others, they have a haunting feeling that they ought to be giving more time to prayer. Yet when they are at their prayers, the thought of the vast needs of the world presses upon them and they feel that they ought to be working.

In attempting to reconcile this contradiction, people try to accompany their work with mental prayers; they try to work and pray at the same time. But this proves to be distracting. Some forms of physical exercise, largely automatic — walking at an even pace, for example — readily admit of mental prayer, but most household tasks and almost all skilled labor require fixed attention, the concentration of the mind on the movement of the hands, and to try to think words of prayer at the same time causes distraction and confusion of thought. It is difficult to do two things thoroughly well at the same time. The Fathers of the Desert used to weave mats and meditate, but weaving mats probably required as little attention as knitting, or folding circulars.

The solution may be found in what we will call "acted prayer." In this, the act itself becomes a prayer — that is to say, the will that carries on the work is directed toward God in the movement of the hands and so forth, just as the will that stimulates vocal prayer is directed toward God in coherent thoughts and sentences.

In acted prayer, no attempt is made to think of God or to address words to Him, but the will enters upon the work as a *means of uniting ourselves with God in doing, carefully and deftly, what will be pleasing to Him.* It will be seen that such a prayer as this, so far from interfering with one's work, makes the very work a prayer. Something like this was probably in the mind of George Herbert when he wrote the well-known lines:

Teach me, my God and King,
In all things Thee to see,
And what I do in anything,
To do it as for Thee.

All may of Thee partake,
Nothing can be so mean
Which with this tincture (for Thy sake)
Will not grow bright and clean.
A servant with this clause
Makes drudgery divine:
Who sweeps a room, as for Thy cause,
Makes that and the action fine.

This is the famous stone
That turneth all to gold:
For that which God doth touch and own
Cannot for less be told.

Prayers at night

The circumstances of people differ widely. Some persons will find the evening the occasion of greatest freedom for devotion; for others it is almost always a crowded time. But for all there are three forms of prayer that should

find place at the close of the day, besides the commendation on lying down. The natural time for these would be
just before retiring, but it is suggested that, if one is likely
to be kept up late, the night prayers should be said immediately after the evening meal — when there is apt to be a
breathing space — leaving only the commendation to be
made on going to bed.

The three forms of night prayers are confession, intercession, and thanksgiving. A few words as to each of these
must suffice.

Confession

For this, it will be necessary to give a few minutes to
self-examination as to the doings of the day just ended,
seeking the illumination of the Holy Spirit to enable you
to see where you have been guilty of failure and sin in
thought, word, or deed, or in leaving something undone
that should have been performed.

If we have a book for private prayer, it ought to contain
at least half a dozen questions to ask ourselves, questions
that strike at our predominant fault, and bring to mind
the special weaknesses and temptations that have to be
met. The questions should be specific, and framed so that

we can without much delay answer yes or no. For example, "Did I lose my temper with Miss So-and-so today?" "Did I forget to say my prayers at noon?" "Did I give way to gossip?" "Was I square in what I said about securities at the meeting of directors?" The result of this self-examination should be noted down, and then there should be a definite confession of our sins to God, not necessarily spoken out loud, but as clearly worded as though we were telling them to a fellow-creature.

We should then make the Act of Contrition:

> *My God, I am sorry that I have offended Thee,*
> *who art so good; forgive me for Jesus' sake,*
> *and I will try to sin no more.*

⌒

Intercession

This is a very large subject; it might well by itself take up a whole volume. What is apposite to be said here is that each of us should have a list of persons and of intentions for which we pray every night, and others for which we pray once a week and some that we remember on special days once a year. *And this list should be changed from time to time,* some names dropped and others written in. We should pray for "the holy Church throughout all the world," for the diocese and the bishop, for the parish and its priest, for missions and missionaries, and for the vast needs of the world. Then there would be our relatives and friends, living and departed and those under our care.

⌒

Thanksgiving

Thirdly, we should give thanks to God, for His loving-kindness and mercy, for the eternal Son coming to be Man, for His saving the world by His Cross, for the Church in which the Holy Spirit brings us forgiveness of sins and unites us with God. And, then, for special blessings: for strength to serve, for patience to endure, for the kindness of friends, for the discipline of pain, for deliverance in temptation, for a loving smile from the face of some little child.

This matter of thanksgiving, again, is one that would repay extended treatment. It is one of the forms of prayer most often neglected, and with unhappy results of peevishness and self-pity. Just as prayer for others purges out the spirit that leads us to criticize and censure others, so thanksgiving drives away the ugly spirit of grumbling and complaint.

The Work of Prayer

⮟

Commendation

Lastly, as we lie down to rest, and sleep comes on, it should find us commending our souls to God, releasing the strain of life in the embrace of the Everlasting Arms, our last thought being of Him who has been with us all the day, with whom we hope to be throughout eternity:

Into Thy hands I commend my spirit,
for Thou hast redeemed me,
O Lord, Thou God of truth.

I will lay me down in peace and
take my rest, for it is Thou, Lord, only
who enablest us to dwell in safety.

Chapter Nine

Be Prepared for Difficulties in Prayer

"No one is likely to do much at prayer
who does not look upon it as a work
to be prepared for and entered upon
with all the serious earnestness
which a difficult task demands."

Bishop Hamilton

Prayer is the hardest work in the world. That does not mean that only a very few people can do it, as only such persons as Joseph Scaliger and Thomas Babington Macaulay could memorize a book at a single reading. Anyone can pray, *if* he will pay the price. A little child can pray. A man handicapped by the sins of a lifetime can pray, if he will give the sins up. A dying soul can pray, even when the lips can no longer move or the voice sound.

Yet it is still true to say that prayer is the hardest work in the world. For true and acceptable prayer requires the sacrifice of one's self, and that is the most expensive of all surrender. Even Satan himself knows that: "Skin for skin; yea, all that a man hath will he give for his life."[54] Our blessed Lord discloses it: "If any man will come after me, let him deny [i.e., give up all claim to] himself."[55] St. Paul

[54] Job 2:4.
[55] Matt. 16:24.

bears witness to it: "You are not your own; you are bought with a great price"[56] — the price of the Blood of God. As has been said, "It does not take much of a man to be a Christian, but it takes all the man is."[57]

To recall what has been said earlier, the heart of all prayers is "Thy will be done," and that requires the unconditional surrender of our own will. "No man can serve two masters."[58] If we serve God, we cannot at the same time be governed by self-will, or live to please ourselves.

What stifles prayer

To illustrate this in several particulars:

Let us first consider some of the things that would render any true prayer impossible.

One of these is a state of impenitence for a mortal sin a person has committed. Perhaps the most comprehensive definition of prayer is "the moving of the will toward God with the desire to know Him better and to love Him more." But sin, mortal sin at any rate, is the turning of the

---

[56] Cf. 1 Cor. 6:19-20.

[57] Thomas Huxley.

[58] Matt. 6:24.

will away from God, the averting of the heart from Him. And just as it is impossible to go two opposite ways with the body, so it is impossible to go two opposite ways with the soul. You cannot at the same time go both north and south. You may go north first, and south afterward, or south first and north afterward, as you sometimes see an irresolute person twisting and turning about, as first one and then another impulse sways him. But you can go only one way at a time.

So in some bitter struggle with temptation, we may pray to do right and then yield to the temptation and will to do wrong. But while we are really praying, we are not consenting to sin. That is why a life of prayer is a life of union with God. We can do anything else, even to receiving the Blessed Sacrament with the lips, and yet continue in alienation from God; but we cannot persevere in prayer and continue to resist the Holy Spirit. "No man can say Lord Jesus, but by the Holy Spirit,"[59] and so if we do but say the Holy Name with faith and loyalty and love, the Holy Spirit moves us to it.

This is not always perceived. As a powerful writer has pointed out, a man may persist in a habit of mortal sin,

[59] Cf. 1 Cor. 12:3.

falling into it from time to time, yet *between* the falls may seem to pray earnestly and effectively, and even in other respects to make progress.

But, as the writer goes on to say, although "there may be cases where an earnest effort is being made to cure some long-standing fault of character, and to break the chain of past sins, yet, generally speaking, the state of things described above, in which frequent and recurrent sin has little or no effect to shake prayer, or spoil the joy of religion, is a most deadly and dangerous one. . . . Ask yourself earnestly whether your sins have ceased to hinder your religion. And if you are bound to answer that it is so, then be horribly afraid. For be sure of this: that if your sins have ceased to hinder your religion, then your religion has ceased to hinder your sins. And that is the surest sign of a soul 'dead in trespasses and sins,' or, at best, in mortal peril."

More often, thank God, the inability to pray is the proof to the soul itself that it is out of harmony with God. As the same writer says, "Try to pray when you are full of angry, selfish, impure, or revengeful thoughts, and you will prove for yourself the truth of the psalmist's words: 'If I incline unto wickedness with mine heart, the Lord will not hear me.' "

Be Prepared for Difficulties in Prayer

"Fruitless" prayers

A different obstacle presents itself when a person has been praying for a long time for what he feels *must* be the will of God, as for the conversion of a soul, or for the recovery from illness of one whose life seems necessary for the carrying on of some good work, and still no result can be discerned. Here the question that forces itself upon the mind is: "Why does not God answer my prayer? I seem to have fulfilled the requisite conditions. I believe in His power and His love. I am trying to do His will. I am in charity with all the world. And yet my prayer seems fruitless."

Now here certain distinctions are necessary.

First, if we are praying for the submission of another to the will of God, for his abandonment of some sin or his performance of some righteous action, we must remember that there are limitations to what God Himself can do. When we confess that God is "almighty," we do not mean that He can do all things. It is impossible for God to lie, or to give His approval to anything that is opposed to His moral nature, to His justice, holiness, and love. And since God has limited Himself by creating other wills than His own, He cannot act as though those wills did not exist.

The Work of Prayer

God cannot do what is inconsistent with His own appointed order. He cannot make a thing both to be and not to be at the same time. He cannot make a human being without a will, or take that will away and leave him a human being.

When we pray that another may make a right choice, we do not pray that God will take from the person the power to choose; and the person might persist in choosing wrongly. What we can do is still to pray, "Thy will be done" and ask that God will deal with the wayward soul in His own infinite patience and tenderness and love, but also in accordance with His own truth and righteousness and justice.

Second, if we are praying for some temporal good to come to another, or to many others, however desirable that good may seem to us, we must recognize our ignorance of how the purpose of God can best be carried out. When, in times of persecution, Christians were dragged to their death, no doubt their fellow Christians prayed with utmost earnestness that they might escape. Sometimes, as in the case of St. Peter when the company in John Mark's house were praying for him, God set His servant free. But sometimes, as in the case of St. Stephen, the enemies of the Church had their way. Yet in answer to the dying prayer and willing sacrifice of St. Stephen, Saul the perse-cutor became St. Paul the Apostle of the Nations, and St. Peter himself at length died a witness for his Master.

"The blood of the martyrs is the seed of the harvest." "Imagine all martyrdom blotted from the world's history, how blank and barren were the page!"

So with all temporal calamities; God can use them to His glory, and to His people's good. "All things work together for good to them that love God,"[60] and the sovereign will of God can use all the events and circumstances of time to further His plans. "All things serve Thee." Wherever Satan seems to have scored a victory, there will be, in answer to the prayers of His people, in God's own time, the scene of his signal overthrow and defeat. The treachery of Judas contributed to the redemption of the world.

Lastly, one must see that the delay to grant our petitions for ourselves might be due to the fact that our perseverance in the prayer is necessary for our own growth in the knowledge of God, and our fuller response in faith and hope and love toward Him.

St. Augustine says, "By delaying to grant our petitions, God increases our desires. By increasing our desires, God

[60] Rom. 8:28.

enlarges our heart. By enlarging our heart, God prepares us to be filled with Himself."

"No man rises from his prayer a better man but he has received an answer to his petition," and there is one experience that many have had which is most reassuring. It is to kneel down and pray — it may be in a veritable agony — for something that we feel God *must* give us because we *must* have it, and yet to get up entirely willing to go without it.

Special petitions

What was said in the last section might lead some persons to take up an attitude that would go far to paralyze prayer. Such persons would say, "If God's will can so overrule all things to His purpose, and compel even the wicked to further His plans, then why should we make any special requests of Him? Why not confine ourselves to saying, 'Thy will be done' and leave all to Him?"

But that would be to forget that God has placed in us manifold desires, desires for such things as are fitted to meet our needs and to bring us happiness and joy. God does not want us to extinguish those desires, to grow indifferent and apathetic to the richness and beauty of creation, to blind ourselves to the glory of the sunlight and the love in human hearts. That is the error of Buddhistic asceticism, and Puritan rigorism.

We are not to drop God's good gifts out of our hands in sour contempt, as if to say, "Oh, I don't care for it. I can get along very well without it. I won't ask God for anything; then I shall not be disappointed if He does not let me have it."

This may sound submissive, but it comes from "the pride that apes humility."[61] The truly childlike spirit would rather foster the desires for the good things God has made and say, "O Father, it is very beautiful and dear. Give it to me if it be Thy will; yet if it seems best to Thee that I should not have it now, or keep it when I have it, then I would lay it in Thy hand to keep it for me until I am ready for it, in this world or the next. Beyond and above all other desires is my desire that Thou shouldst do what Thou knowest to be best. 'Not my will but Thine be done.' "

Then we shall see more and more that no created good is good in and by itself, but because it comes to us as a token of our Father's love and as a channel of His grace; that

[61] Samuel Taylor Coleridge.

"the gift without the giver is bare"; that while we ask, and rightly ask, for the gift, we should ask also for grace to use it as the means to a closer union with God; and that if God takes away the desire of our eyes at a stroke, it is so that He may give Himself to us still more directly and more fully. And we shall learn to say, not, "I have labored in vain; I have spent my strength for naught,"[62] but "The Lord gave and the Lord hath taken away; blessed be the Name of the Lord."[63]

[62] Cf. Isa. 49:4.
[63] Job 1:21.

Chapter Ten

Understand Why You Should Pray

"Prayer can obtain everything; it can open
the windows of Heaven, and shut the gates
of Hell; it can put a holy restraint upon God,
and detain an angel till he leave a blessing."

Jeremy Taylor

⌒

"It is as natural for a boy to pray as to play ball." Yes, if we had the hearts of children we should not find ourselves asking, "Why should I pray?" But to most of us, sooner or later, that question comes. It may be, as was said in the previous chapter, because prayer seems needless; it may be because it has begun to seem fruitless.

Let us, then, set down some of the reasons why, according to the bidding of the apostle, we should not cease to pray; why, as our blessed Lord teaches, "men ought always to pray and not to faint."[64]

⌒

God wants to hear us

First, we should pray because God loves us and wants us to be in intimate relation with Him as His friends. "God's love and man's response — that is the summary of

[64] Luke 18:1.

our life as Christians. And it is God's love, the kindness of God our Savior, that comes first; we love Him because He first loved us."

It is really very awful to face the contrast: on the one hand, that it does make a difference to God whether or not we speak to Him; yes, that the Heart of Jesus is hungry for a word from us; and on the other hand, that we so lightly forget or omit our prayers, or "say" them so heedlessly that it must hurt our Lord almost more than if we had not gone through the half-empty form.

At any rate, here is the first constraining motive for prayer.

> "Not for the sake of gaining aught,
>   Not seeking a reward;
>   But as Thyself hast loved me,
>   O ever-loving Lord.[65]

⌒

Prayer allows us to "help" God

Second, we should pray in order to "help" God. The expression might sound rude or rash. It would be so, if we

[65] Edward Caswall.

meant by it that we are not dependent upon God, that we could cooperate with Him on a level of equality, as one man may help another. But this it not what is meant.

In His incomprehensible love for us, God has gone so far as to limit His omnipotence by making each of us able to *choose* whether or not we will work along with Him. We can do nothing to help God except by the strength that He Himself supplies. But we can *will* that He should use us. And it is by prayer that we let God take our wills and work through them. Remember, the heart of all prayer is "Thy will be done." Our prayer is not to alter the divine scheme, but to ask those things which God has decreed "should be brought about by prayer."

When we are in anxiety over some dear, willful child, it heartens us to know that one whom we trust and revere is praying for him. We do not think that he loves the child more than God does, or that he alone, apart from God, can bring a blessing to the child, but we are glad to feel that God's love for the child is in his heart, that our friend is a "worker together with God" on his behalf. So should we, all of us, be fellow-laborers with God by prayer.

And since we were created for fellowship with one another as well as with God, therefore we help God most when we combine with one another by the Holy Spirit in united prayer. Jesus said, "If two of you shall consent upon earth, concerning anything whatsoever they shall ask, it shall be done for them by my Father who is in Heaven. For where there are two or three gathered together in my name, there am I in the midst of them."[66]

◌

Prayer allows us to help others

Third, we should pray in order to help others. This is, of course, really the same as our second reason for prayer. Only, then we were thinking of prayer as the way in which our wills cooperate with God. Now we are thinking of how, in prayer, our wills grapple with other souls to draw them to Him. The Christian, in his intercession for his brother, holds up one hand to be clasped in the strong, nail-pierced hand of Christ and stretches his other hand out to grasp his brother, sinking, it may be, in the quicksand of temptation. And in prayer we can pursue and overtake those who have baffled our every other attempt to reach them.

And, while prayer is our surest way of helping others, it is also the safest way, in that no true prayer can bring harm

[66] Matt. 18:19-20.

to another soul. "Say little about God to others, and much about others to God" is a wise rule, although there are times when we must speak to others of God if we would not be cowardly and cruel. Yet, however carefully we choose the words we say to others, those words may be mistaken, and our most loving overtures may be misunderstood. But it is impossible for God to misunderstand us, or to let anything we say to Him, however mistakenly (provided we are humble and sincere), lead to His inflicting injury upon those for whom we pray. And here, again, it is united prayer in which we "agree" together, however outwardly separated, that does most for others.

⸎

Prayer wins help for us

Fourth, we should pray in order to win help for ourselves: forgiveness for our frequent offenses, strength to resist temptation, light in perplexity, grace to undertake some work to which God calls us. Our Lord gives very implicit instruction as to this reason for prayer. "Ask, and it shall be given you; seek, and you shall find; knock and it shall be opened to you."[67] There is no niggardliness on the

[67] Matt. 7:7.

part of God. He would not have us "lack anything that is good."[68] But, although all we have comes from Him, He makes the condition that we should pray for His gifts (in general or in particular), in order that we may look to Him as the Giver and receive His gifts as tokens of His fatherly love.

So the farmer cannot fashion the tiniest seed, cannot make the sun shine or the rain fall or the south wind blow. He must look to God for all these His gifts. Yet the farmer must plow and sow and cultivate, or there will be no harvest when September comes.

⌒

Prayer builds up the fellowship

Fifth, we must pray because thereby we unite ourselves with our brothers and sisters in the "blessed company of all faithful people," and so build up the fellowship everywhere. The Christian never prays alone. He is always a member of the Body of Christ, and he prays by the Holy Spirit, who fills that Body and makes his prayer one with the great torrent of supplication ever pouring up to the Throne of God.

[68] Cf. Ps. 33:11 (RSV = Ps. 34:10).

Yet, also, there are some forms of prayer impossible to the Christian save in actual company with others. Above all there is the great eucharistic offering, wherein, day by day, Christ, by the oblation of Himself, "makes His immense act of love for His own great ends and the vast needs of souls." The altar is the focus of all the prayers we offer in Christ, by His Holy Spirit. And every earnest pleading in prayer, alone or with others, draws us together in Him.

☞

At the beginning of this little treatise, we thought that it was by prayer that we take and keep our place in the spiritual world of living spirits who have their center in God. God made us for this very thing, that we might know and love Him, might be in fellowship with Him and with others in and through Him. God desires this, with a longing as much beyond our thought as He is greater than we are. He wants each one of us, personally, individually, to be in conscious, loving communion with Him.

Prayers for Every Day

BASIC PRAYERS

Our Father, who art in Heaven,
hallowed by Thy Name.
Thy kingdom come. Thy will be done,
on earth as it is in Heaven.
Give us this day our daily bread.
And forgive us our trespasses,
as we forgive those who trespass against us.
And lead us not into temptation,
but deliver us from evil.
Amen

Hail Mary, full of grace,
the Lord is with thee.
Blessed art thou among women,
and blessed is the fruit of thy womb, Jesus.
Holy Mary, Mother of God,
pray for us sinners,
now and at the hour of our death.
Amen

The Work of Prayer

Glory be to the Father
and to the Son
and to the Holy Spirit,
as it was in the beginning,
is now, and ever shall be,
world without end.
Amen

Prayers for Every Day

MORNING PRAYERS

☞

Prayer on Rising
I praise my God this day;
I give myself to God this day;
I ask God to help me this day.

☞

*Read at least five verses
from Scripture, particularly from
the Gospels or the Psalms*

☞

Examination of Forethought

☞

Act of Faith
My God, I believe in Thee, and all that
Thy Church doth teach, because Thou
hast said it, and Thy word is true.

The Work of Prayer

⁓

Act of Hope
My God, I hope in Thee for grace and
for glory, because of Thy mercy,
Thy promises, and Thy power.

⁓

Act of Love
My God, I love Thee, and for Thy sake
I desire to love my neighbor as myself.

⁓

Kyrie
Lord, King and Father unbegotten,
True Essence of the Godhead, have mercy on us.
Lord, Fount of light and Creator of all things,
have mercy on us.
Lord, Thou who hast signed us with the
seal of Thine image, have mercy on us.
Christ, True God and True Man,
have mercy on us.
Christ, Rising Sun, through whom are
all things, have mercy on us.
Christ, Perfection of Wisdom, have mercy on us.

Lord, vivifying Spirit and power of
life, have mercy on us.
Lord, Breath of the Father and the Son,
in Whom are all things, have mercy on us.
Lord, Purger of sin and Almoner of grace,
we beseech Thee, abandon us not
because of our Sins,
O Consoler of the sorrowing
soul, have mercy on us.

⌒

Apostles' Creed
I believe in God,
the Father Almighty,
Creator of Heaven and earth;
and in Jesus Christ, His only Son, our Lord,
who was conceived by the Holy Spirit,
born of the Virgin Mary, suffered under Pontius
Pilate, was crucified, died, and was buried.
He descended into Hell; the third day
He rose again from the dead;
He ascended into Heaven and is seated
at the right hand of God, the Father Almighty;

from thence He shall come to
judge the living and the dead.
I believe in the Holy Spirit,
the holy Catholic Church,
the Communion of Saints,
the forgiveness of sins,
the resurrection of the body,
and life everlasting. Amen.

NOON PRAYERS

Angelus[69]

V. The Angel of the Lord declared unto Mary.
R. And she conceived of the Holy Spirit.
Hail Mary. . . .

V. Behold the handmaid of the Lord.
R. Be it done unto me according to thy word.
Hail Mary. . . .

V. And the Word was made Flesh.
R. And dwelt among us.
Hail Mary. . . .

V. Pray for us, O holy Mother of God.
R. That we may be made
worthy of the promises of Christ.

Let us pray: Pour forth, we beseech Thee, O Lord,
Thy grace into our hearts, that we to whom the
Incarnation of Christ Thy Son was made known by

[69] The Angelus is traditionally recited in the morning (six
o'clock), at noon, and in the evening (six o'clock).

the message of an angel, may by His Passion and
Cross be brought to the glory of His Resurrection.
Through the same Christ Our Lord. Amen.

Salvator Mundi
O Savior of the world, who by Thy Cross
and Precious Blood hast redeemed us, save us,
and help us, we humbly beseech Thee, O Lord.

NIGHT PRAYERS

☞

Examination of Conscience

☞

Act of Contrition

My God, I am sorry that I have offended Thee,
who art so good; forgive me for Jesus' sake,
and I will try to sin no more.

☞

Intercessions

☞

Thanksgiving

☞

Commendation

Into Thy hands I commend my spirit, for
Thou hast redeemed me, O Lord, Thou
God of truth. I will lay me down in peace
and take my rest, for it is Thou, Lord,
only who enablest us to dwell in safety.

Examination-of-Conscience Questions

Examination-of-Conscience Questions

Personal Intentions

Personal Intentions

Personal Intentions

Personal Intentions

Personal Intentions

~

James O. S. Huntington
(1854-1935)

James Otis Sargent Huntington studied at Harvard and at St Andrew's Divinity School in Syracuse before being ordained around 1880. Although an Anglican priest, he was drawn to the spirituality of the Catholic Church and even founded the Order of the Holy Cross, a monastic order based on the spirituality of St. Benedict. Members of this order engage in parish work and social work.

Along with serving as superior of the order, Fr. Huntington devoted himself to prayer, preaching, teaching, and counseling.

Please send your tax-deductible contribution to the address below.

For your free catalog,
call toll-free: **1-800-888-9344**

Sophia Institute Press®
Box 5284
Manchester, NH 03108
www.sophiainstitute.com